Birds

Gillian Doherty

Designed by Neil Francis

Illustrated by John Woodcock
Consultant: Dr. S. James Reynolds, Edward Grey Institute of Field
Ornithology, Department of Zoology, University of Oxford

Cover: bald eagle
Title page: flamingoes
This page: white-faced whistling ducks

Contents

A European robin

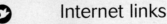

Internet links

For links to the websites recommended in this book, go to the **Usborne Quicklinks Website** at **www.usborne-quicklinks.com** and enter the keywords "discovery birds". Usborne Publishing is not responsible for the content on any website other than its own. Please read the internet safety guidelines on the Usborne Quicklinks Website and on page 62 of this book.

★ Pictures in this book with a star symbol beside them can be downloaded for your own personal use from the Usborne Quicklinks Website

What is a bird? . . . .

A bird is an animal with feathers and wings. Most birds can fly, although there are some that can't. Birds are found all over the world – in hot deserts, icy polar regions and high up on mountains.

Bird types

There are over 9,000 different kinds, or species, of birds. Within each species, birds have similar patterns and body shapes.

The number of species we know about is still growing, as scientists discover new species in remote places, or identify differences between birds they thought were the same species.

Feather functions

All birds are covered in overlapping feathers. Some types of feathers keep them warm, while others help them to fly. Feathers are made of a substance called keratin, which is what people's nails and hair are made of too.

Legs and wings

Many animals have four legs, but birds only have two. Instead of front legs, birds have wings. All birds have wings, even those that can't fly.

This is a lilac-breasted roller. All birds have a similar basic body shape to this.

Internet links

For links to websites where you can see pictures of many different birds from around the world and learn how to identify birds, go to **www.usborne-quicklinks.com**

Other flying animals

Some insects, such as flies and bees, can fly. However, the only mammals that can fly are bats. Like birds, they fly by flapping their wings and can stay in the air for a long time.

Colugos, flying squirrels and flying lizards have flaps of skin between their front and back legs. They stretch these out so that they can glide between trees, but they can't really fly.

This long-eared bat has large, leathery wings.

These long bones which support the wings are actually the bat's fingers.

Starting as eggs

Birds don't give birth to live young as some animals do. They lay eggs, from which their babies hatch. Reptiles, such as snakes and crocodiles, also lay eggs.

A grass snake curled around its eggs

Beaks

Birds have hard beaks, but their mouths are soft and fleshy inside. They use their beaks to pick things up because they don't have hands.

The saddlebill stork uses its impressive beak to scoop up fish.

Fact: The earliest known bird-like creature was Archaeopteryx, which had feathers like a bird's but a skull like a reptile's. It lived around 130 million years ago.

Flying machines

Birds are the perfect flying machines. A bird's feathers, wings and body shape all help it to take to the air. Birds fly to escape from enemies, to travel to warmer places and to search for food.

Body shape

Birds have streamlined bodies, which enable them to slip easily through the air.

Lightweights

If birds are too big and heavy, they can't fly. Even the biggest flying birds are much, much lighter than other animals of the same size. This is because they have hollow bones.

At around 10kg (22lbs), the mute swan is one of the heaviest birds that can fly.

A mallard duck is about the same size as a rabbit, but it weighs about half as much.

Flight muscles

Birds have large, strong chest muscles. These give them the power to flap their wings repeatedly for a long time.

Internet links

For links to websites where you can investigate the unique features of bird feathers and skeletons and find out how a bird flaps its wings, go to **www.usborne-quicklinks.com**

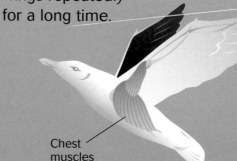

Chest muscles

★

Fact: Over a fifth of a bird's body-weight can be made up of flight muscles.

Wings

A bird's wings are rounded on top and curved underneath. This shape is called an aerofoil. As the air passes around the wing, the air above presses down less than the air below. This helps to lift the bird as it flaps its wings.

The red arrows on this diagram show the path of the air as it passes around the bird's wing.

Tiptop feathers

The condition of a bird's feathers is very important for flight. Birds use their beaks to straighten out and clean their feathers. This is called preening. As a bird's feathers wear out, they are regularly replaced with new ones.

A gannet preening its feathers

Flight feathers

The large feathers that make up most of a bird's wings and tail are called flight feathers. As these strong, stiff feathers push down on the air during flight, they help the bird gain height.

Flying high

Birds fly by flapping, gliding, soaring or hovering. Their type of flight depends upon their body size, wing shape and how far and fast they have to travel.

Flapping

The main way birds stay in the air is by flapping their wings. They use their wings both to propel themselves along and to rise up in the air. This is called gaining lift.

Wing size

Many small birds have to flap their wings quickly to stay in the air. Birds with bigger, broader wings don't need to flap their wings as often, because the wing's larger surface area provides more power as it pushes down on the air.

This European robin has small, rounded wings, which it flaps very quickly as it flies.

Eight shape

To fly, birds don't just beat their wings up and down. Instead, they move the tips of the wings in the shape of the number eight.

The bird gains lift by pushing down on the air.

The feathers open to let the air through as the wings move up.

The feathers close ready to push down.

The wings push down once again.

Flying in circles

Sometimes you may see birds flying around and around in circles. They are using rising spirals of warm air, called thermals, to carry them. This way of flying is called soaring.

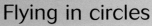

A bird soaring in a spiral movement

Gliding

Birds can stay in the air for a long time without flapping their wings. This is called gliding. To do this, they keep their wings stiff and allow the wind to carry them along.

Albatrosses have long, narrow wings, which are good for gliding.

Hovering

Some birds can hover in the air in one spot. They do this by angling their bodies and flapping their wings very quickly.

Hummingbirds are well known for flying like this, but other birds, such as kestrels, sometimes use a similar technique when hunting.

To stay in one place, a kestrel brings its tail forward and makes very small wing movements.

Internet links

For links to websites where you can watch animations showing how birds take off, flap their wings and glide through the air, go to **www.usborne-quicklinks.com**

Flying style

Different species of birds often have distinctive ways of flying, and you may even be able to identify birds from a distance by the way they fly.

The six stages of this photograph were taken in quick succession. They show a Java dove building up height after take-off.

  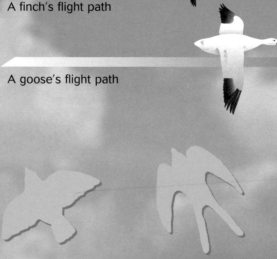

Take-off

Some birds take off from a standstill by leaping into the air and beating their wings vigorously. However, many larger birds need to take a short run up before they can take off. For example, swans and geese use water as a runway to build up speed.

Flight patterns

As birds fly, their flight paths are often quite recognizable. For example, many small birds, such as tits and finches, rise and dip as they fly, whereas ducks and geese keep a fairly level flight.

A finch's flight path

A goose's flight path

Wing shape

Birds have wings that are shaped to suit different types of flight or different environmental conditions.

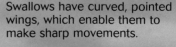

Eagles have big, broad wings, which are good for gliding and soaring.

Jays have short, blunt wings, which enable them to fly among trees easily.

Swallows have curved, pointed wings, which enable them to make sharp movements.

Landing trouble

Landing is very tricky as birds have to slow down quickly, but remain in full control as they do so. Small birds are highly skilled at landing, but larger birds find it more difficult.

Slowing down

To slow down, birds angle their wings and bring their feet and tail feathers forward, tilting the body. Together, these act like brakes.

This great tit is swinging its feet and lower body forward ready to land on a bird feeder.

Skydiving

Birds of prey dive rapidly through the air in pursuit of other birds or small mammals. They do this by folding back their wings so that they don't drag through the air.

When hunting for prey, peregrine falcons are the fastest-flying birds.

Legs and feet .....

The feet of different species of birds vary a lot, depending on where the birds live and what they use their feet for. Birds' feet are important for landing, walking, perching, catching or holding food, and swimming.

A weaver bird using its feet to grip tightly onto a branch

Walking on tiptoes

At first glance, it looks as though birds' knees bend the opposite way from people's. In fact, what looks like the knee is the ankle. So birds actually walk on their toes. Birds may have two, three or four toes.

Body balance

Most of a bird's weight is at the front of its body. This makes the position and structure of the legs important, because they help balance and stability.

This Cape white-eye has no difficulty balancing on a tiny branch.

This is the bird's ankle.

Internet links

For a link to a website where you can find out more about birds' feet, see birds' skulls, find out more about what birds eat and even dissect a virtual owl pellet, go to
www.usborne-quicklinks.com

Fact: A group of birds called perching birds can clamp their feet around branches so firmly that, even while the birds are sleeping, they don't lose their grip.

Paddling

Many waterbirds, such as ducks and swans, have webbed feet, with a piece of skin stretching between each toe. They use their feet like paddles to propel them through the water.

A duck uses its feet to push against the water.

A great spotted woodpecker can grip a tree trunk even though there's nothing for it to wrap its feet around.

Feet for walking

Birds such as emus and ostriches, that spend all of their time on the ground, need feet that are suited to walking and running. An ostrich's foot has two large toes that provide stability during movement.

Ostriches are the only birds with just two toes.

Getting a grip

Birds that climb, such as parrots and woodpeckers, need a good grip. Many of them have two toes pointing forward and two pointing backward, so that they can cling firmly to tree trunks as they feed.

Beaks and eating..........

Birds use their beaks (also known as bills) to catch, grab and carry their food. They don't have teeth, so they usually have to break their food into chunks before they eat it.

Food that fits the bill

Birds eat all kinds of food, from insects, fish and animals to seeds and fruit. The size and shape of their beaks are often suited to the kinds of food they eat. Here are some examples of how they use them.

A toucan uses its long beak to reach up into trees for food.

Crossbills' beaks have overlapping tips, which they use to force open pine cones.

Pelicans have pouch-like beaks, which expand to scoop up fish.

This ground hornbill has caught an insect by using its long beak like pincers.

Food mixers

Birds can't chew their food because they don't have teeth, so they swallow it in chunks. The food is ground up by strong muscles in the bird's gizzard, which is just below the stomach.

Some birds deliberately swallow grit and tiny stones. These line the gizzard, creating a rough surface that helps to grind down tough food such as seeds.

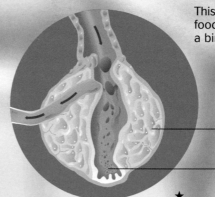

This diagram shows food passing through a bird's gizzard.

Muscular walls of gizzard

The food is ground up here.

★

This tiny mouse seems unaware of the tawny owl swooping silently down on it.

Down in one

When owls and hawks eat small animals, they swallow the fur and bones as well as the flesh. Their bodies can't process these parts, so they are held in the gizzard. Later the bird coughs them up in a tightly-packed ball called a pellet.

You can see the animal bones in this owl pellet.

Fact: The brown pelican scoops up water in its bill when fishing. Its bill can hold about a bucketful of water.

15

Senses.....................

Some birds, particularly those that hunt other animals, have very powerful senses, which help them to find food from high in the air when flying.

Bald eagles have very good eyesight.

All around vision

Most birds have eyes on the sides of their heads. This enables them to see nearly all the way around them without moving. The clearest areas are those they focus on with both eyes at the same time. This is called binocular vision, and it is how people see.

The shaded area shows the area that a sparrow can see without moving its head.

This is the area of binocular vision.

What big eyes

Birds have huge eyes in relation to their body size. For example, an eagle's eyes are about the same size as yours, although its body is much smaller.

Most birds have very good sight. They can see distant objects very clearly, even when the objects are moving quickly.

Extra eyelids

Birds have extra eyelids that are semi-transparent. These protect the eyes and can sweep across to keep the eyes clean. They move from left to right, not top to bottom like the main eyelids. Some birds that swim underwater use these eyelids like swimming goggles, allowing them to keep their eyes open underwater.

This is a close-up of a white-bellied sea-eagle's eye without the extra eyelid over it.

This shows the same eye as above, but it has the extra eyelid covering it.

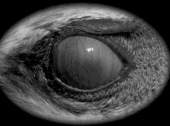

Sniffing out food

We know little about birds' sense of smell. Vultures can find dead animals from high in the sky, even when they are hidden. This may be because they can smell them.

Kiwis are thought to have a very good sense of smell. While most birds have nostrils at the end of the beak that is closest to the head, kiwis' nostrils are at the tip, so they can sniff out worms and insects on the ground.

Vultures may be able to smell food even if it is hidden by trees or bushes.

Sensitive beaks

Wading birds have touch sensors at the ends of their beaks. These help them to feel the movement of worms and insects in mud or water, even if they can't see them.

Hearing

Birds can hear a wide range of sounds and some can distinguish up to 6,000 separate sounds every second. Birds that hunt at night have particularly good hearing, allowing them to locate prey precisely even though it is dark.

 Internet links

For links to websites where you can read about birds' senses and find fascinating facts and close-up pictures of birds' eyes, go to **www.usborne-quicklinks.com**

This yellow-billed stork is feeling for insects using sensors in its beak.

Finding a mate

Birds have to find a mate (a bird of the opposite sex) in order to produce chicks. Some species of birds have lots of mates, while others have just one partner for their entire lives. Birds go to amazing lengths to attract the attention of a possible mate.

Opposites attract

It is usually the male birds who have to impress the females. For this reason, they often have brighter, more elaborate feathers. Many males spread out their feathers so that they can show them off.

Male bonding

Some male birds, such as birds-of-paradise and sage grouse, gather in groups so that the females can wander among them and choose the bird they like most. The place where the birds gather is called a lek.

In some species of birds, the males fight to be noticed. But in other species, they care more about how attractive they look as a group.

The Raggiana bird-of-paradise has very flamboyant feathers. This one is swinging upside-down as part of its display.

Song and dance

Some birds sing or dance to attract attention. For example, blue-footed boobies have bright blue feet that they lift up as they dance. They do this so that the female knows they are blue-footed boobies and not red-footed boobies, another species.

A blue-footed booby dancing to attract a mate

Bower builders

An example of how a bowerbird's bower might look

★

Male bowerbirds work very hard to make a good impression. They build elaborate structures called bowers, and decorate them with bright objects such as petals, feathers and berries. The female tours the bowers and chooses the male with the most impressive bower.

Balloon bird

During the mating season the male frigatebird develops a bright red pouch under his chin, which he inflates to attract a mate.

When inflated, the frigatebird's pouch is about the size of a person's head.

Birdsong and calls

Birdsong sounds beautiful but it also has an important purpose. Singing and calling are the main ways that birds communicate with one another.

Sound travels

Many birds live in areas where trees and other vegetation make it difficult for them to see one another. By using sound, they are able to communicate over long distances.

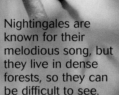

Nightingales are known for their melodious song, but they live in dense forests, so they can be difficult to see.

Singing songs

Songs are usually produced by males. Some are long, complicated tunes, but others can be short and not very musical. Birds belonging to a group known as perching birds are also sometimes known as songbirds.

Male birds sing in order to attract females. Many male songbirds have dull, brown feathers. They don't need bright feathers because they use their voices to make an impression.

Marking territories

Songs intended to attract females are interpreted very differently by other males. By singing, a bird is stating its ownership of a particular area, or territory, and telling other males to stay away.

A wren singing to attract a mate

This is a pied mynah living in the wild in India. In captivity these birds can be taught to speak.

Copycats

Some birds are very good at copying sounds. For example, parrots and mynahs can mimic human speech, lyrebirds can imitate the sound of a chainsaw or a radio, and starlings can make a noise like a telephone ringing.

Internet links

For links to websites where you can find out how birds attract a mate, listen to sound clips of birds singing and see if you can identify different types of bird call, go to
www.usborne-quicklinks.com

Sound machines

Birds produce sounds using a part of their bodies called the syrinx. This contains membranes, like the skin stretched across a drum, which vibrate to produce sound as air is forced past them.

Calls

Calls are short sounds that are made by either males or females. They can be used to show aggression or to warn other birds of dangers nearby. Calls can help a bird to identify its own mate or young in a large group of birds.

A colony of Cape gannets like this can make a lot of noise.

Fact: Lots of birds start to sing just as it grows light in the morning. This is known as the dawn chorus.

Building nests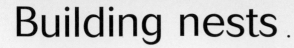

If you see a bird flying along with a twig in its mouth, it is probably building a nest somewhere nearby. Birds build nests so that they have a safe, sheltered place to look after their eggs and bring up their chicks.

All shapes and sizes

Most nests are cup-shaped and built high up in trees. However, they can be built on the ground, on cliff tops or even on chimneys. Nests may also be elaborate shapes, with roofs and entrance tunnels to keep out attackers.

This penduline tit's nest is closed in, so that animals such as snakes can't get in to eat the eggs.

Tools of the trade

Birds use the simplest of tools to build their nests: their beaks and their feet. They use them both to knot and weave the materials together.

This is a weaver bird, hanging from its nest which is made from tightly-knotted grasses.

Building materials

Nests are made from all kinds of materials, from twigs and grasses to silk from spiders' webs and even human hair. Mud and saliva (spit) is often used to cement everything together.

This is an ovenbird's nest. It is made from mud and shaped like an old-fashioned oven.

A soft bed

Birds often line their nests with soft materials, such as feathers, to keep their eggs and chicks warm. They may also dig out a hollow in the nest, so the eggs don't roll around. They do this by turning around in circles.

As the bird turns around in its nest, the weight of its body flattens the materials.

Hoopoes make their nests in trees. This one is bringing food to its young.

Natural nests

Not all birds build nests. Some make burrows or use holes in trees. Others leave their eggs on the ground, but the eggs often blend in with the ground, so they are hard for predators to see.

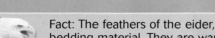 Fact: The feathers of the eider, a type of duck, are sometimes used as bedding material. They are warmer than materials made by people.

Looking after eggs

Some baby animals grow inside their mothers. But if birds carried their babies inside them, they would be too heavy to fly. Instead, their mothers lay eggs and the baby birds grow inside these.

A meadow pipit's egg

What's in an egg?

The hard shell of an egg protects the baby bird inside, and the yolk contains the food that the bird needs to grow.

Egg-shaped

Most eggs are narrower at one end than at the other. Their shape means that they fit together neatly in a nest. Birds that live on cliffs usually lay very pointed eggs. If knocked, these roll in a circle rather than off the ledge.

A great reed warbler's egg

A grasshopper warbler's egg

A redstart's egg

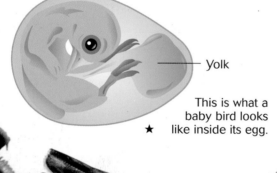
Yolk

This is what a baby bird looks like inside its egg.

Egg numbers

Some birds lay as many as 19 eggs in a batch, or clutch, but others lay just one. A clutch of eggs is usually laid over a period of several days.

Egg care

Eggs have to be kept at the right temperature, or incubated, if the babies inside are to survive. Most birds incubate their eggs by sitting on them. Sometimes it is the male who incubates the eggs and sometimes the female.

This Anna's hummingbird is incubating her eggs by sitting on them.

Mound-makers

Mallee fowls incubate their eggs by burying them in a mound of leaves. As the leaves rot, they give out heat, which keeps the eggs warm.

This mallee fowl is creating a mound to store its eggs. When a chick hatches, it will have to dig its way out of a mound that could be up to 1.5m (5ft) high and 5m (16ft) across.

Rent a nest

Cuckoos lay their eggs in the nests of other birds. The birds think the cuckoo's egg is their own and take care of it.

This cuckoo chick is ejecting the other eggs from its new parents' nest, so that it gets all the food and care.

Good fathers

Emperor penguins lay only one egg. The father incubates the egg by resting it on his feet and covering it with a special fold of skin. This keeps the egg warm and stops it from freezing on the ice. He does this for up to two months, while the female returns to the sea to feed.

The male emperor penguin incubates its egg beneath the fold of skin above his feet.

Internet links

For links to websites where you can see birds' eggs from around the world, find out how birds try to keep their eggs safe and play a nest identification game, go to **www.usborne-quicklinks.com**

Fact: The male emperor penguin does not eat for up to two months while he is incubating an egg.

Baby birds...

When a baby bird is ready to leave its egg, it has to break out through the hard shell. This is called hatching. Some species of birds are more developed than others when they hatch.

Breaking out

Breaking out of an egg from the inside is a difficult job. Chicks have a lump on their beaks, called an egg tooth, which they use to pierce the shell. Chicks call out to their parents shortly before they hatch.

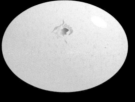
The chick begins by making a small hole in the egg.

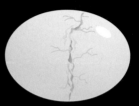
Gradually, it chips all the way around the egg.

Finally, the chick forces the egg apart.

Up and running

Some birds can run around within hours of hatching. This is important for birds that live on the ground, because they are in more danger of being attacked by predators than they would be high in a tree.

This chicken is just one day old, but it is covered in fluffy feathers and can stand up.

Fact: A great tit may make over 900 trips per day to feed its chicks.

Helpless babies

Some chicks don't develop as much as others before they hatch. At first, they may be unable to walk and they may not have feathers. It can take them a long time to develop fully.

This barn owl chick is 18 days old, but it is still unsteady on its feet and not very developed.

Begging for food

When their parents bring food, the chicks open their mouths wide and beg. This is called gaping.

Feeding hungry chicks is a demanding job. Parents have to make many trips each day to find food.

The bright insides of these chicks' mouths show their parents where to drop food.

Internet links

For links to websites where you can see webcam images of an eagle's nest and eggs, or watch a movie of a chick hatching, go to
www.usborne-quicklinks.com

Growing up ....

Before chicks are ready to leave their nests, they have to build up their strength and learn to look after themselves.

These shelduck chicks are keeping close to the adult bird for safety.

Swimming lessons

Chicks are vulnerable to attack during the first few weeks of their lives. As a result, the chicks of many waterbirds develop quickly and are able to swim soon after they hatch. However, they usually stay in close contact with adult birds. For example, shelducks form large groups, or crèches.

Greedy guts

When parents bring food to their chicks, they don't share it out equally. A greedy chick with a loud begging call may get all the food, while a weaker chick may starve.

Nest survival

Some chicks take drastic steps to make sure they get enough food. They may attack and kill weak brothers or sisters, or push eggs out of the nest, so that there is less competition.

The more dominant chick on the right is likely to get the most food.

Flight test

After a few weeks, chicks grow flight feathers, which means they are ready to start flying. They can learn how to flap their wings in the nest, but the only way to learn to fly is by trying it.

A young albatross exercising its wings ready for its first flight

Staying at home

This parent is ignoring its chick to force it to leave the nest.

Even after they are ready to leave their nests, chicks sometimes stay near their parents and beg for food, because this is easier than searching for their own. Parents may be forced to ignore their chicks in order to encourage them to leave and look after themselves.

First flight

Chicks that nest in trees learn to fly by jumping from their nests and flapping their wings. Fortunately, young birds have light, bouncy skeletons. They can fall about 30m (100ft) and still survive. So, if they don't get the hang of flying the first time, they can always try again.

 Internet links

For links to websites where you can chart the growth of baby birds, watch video clips of parents caring for their chicks and find fascinating facts about baby birds, go to **www.usborne-quicklinks.com**

Living in groups

Some species of birds live in groups called colonies, which can contain many thousands of birds. Although these colonies can be overcrowded and noisy, there are advantages to living in large groups.

Gannet groups

Gannets live in groups called gannetries. Families, consisting of two adults and one chick, live only around 80cm (30in) apart, but birds take care not to upset others nearby by venturing onto their patch.

Gannets often live on islands or cliffs, where they are safe from most predators. This means that they don't need to live in groups for protection. But they live in close contact with other gannets because this seems to promote successful breeding.

Within this colony of Cape gannets, you can see pairs of adult birds.

Amazing nests

Sociable weavers often build vast nests that fill entire tree tops. The adult members of the flock all help to build the nest, which is made from dry grass. Each pair of birds has its own small chamber in the nest.

A sociable weavers' nest on a pole

Fact: A sociable weavers' nest can be big enough for up to 300 birds.

Information points

Cliff swallows may use their colonies to exchange information. When some birds find a good food source, the others follow them there. This saves a lot of time and energy looking for food.

This swallow is flying to its nest beneath the cliff. The dark holes are entrances.

🕊 Internet links

For links to websites and video clips about birds that live together in groups, including flamingoes and penguins, go to **www.usborne-quicklinks.com**

Penguin crèches

Macaroni and chinstrap penguins can form groups as large as several hundred thousand birds. Sometimes penguins form crèches, where some parents stay to look after chicks, while others go off to look for food.

Roosting rooks

Rooks usually gather in groups in the late afternoon, ready to settle down for the night. This is known as roosting. The place where they gather is called a rookery. Jackdaws, magpies, carrion crows and ravens may also join them. Different species usually sit in different trees. For example, rooks sit in the taller trees and jackdaws in the shorter ones.

Rooks and jackdaws roosting in trees

Animal partnerships

Some birds develop close relationships with people and other animals. They may help one another to find food or give warnings when predators are approaching.

These birds are red-billed oxpeckers. They are eating insects on the giraffe's neck.

A mobile home

Oxpeckers are found throughout the African grasslands. Entire families of them can live on the back of one animal. They live on large mammals such as giraffes and rhinoceroses, feeding on insects which live or land on the animals' bodies. The animals provide the birds with a convenient way of getting around, and in return the birds may warn them when danger is near.

Internet links

For links to websites with more information and pictures of oxpeckers, egrets, and other birds in Africa, go to **www.usborne-quicklinks.com**

Honeyguides

Birds called honeyguides feed on wax from bees' nests. As a result, they have developed close relationships with animals called ratels, or honey badgers, which feed on honey from the nests.

The honeyguide bird leads the ratel to a nest by making a chattering noise. The ratel breaks open the nest and the honeyguide can then get to the wax more easily.

This ratel is breaking up a bees' nest to get at the honey inside.

After the ratel has finished, the honeyguide eats the wax.

Fact: Each oxpecker can eat up to 2,000 ticks (a type of insect) per day.

Living dangerously

Some birds make their nests close to dangerous animals in the hope of discouraging predators. For example, rufous-naped wrens and bananaquits often nest near wasps. The wasps don't harm them, but they do keep other predators away.

This shows how close to a wasps' nest a bananaquit may build its nest.

Animal with a view

Cattle egrets are often seen on the backs of large animals, such as cows, hippopotamuses and elephants. This gives them a good view of the surrounding landscape and they can feed on ticks that live on the animals' bodies at the same time.

Egrets sometimes follow tractors working on farmland. The movement of the tractors disturbs insects in the soil. When the insects come to the surface, the birds can feed on them.

A cattle egret perched on the head of a hippopotamus

Self protection.........

To escape from danger, most birds fly away rather than put up a fight. But they also have some ingenious ways of defending themselves and outwitting predators.

In disguise

Many birds can avoid being seen by their enemies because their appearance allows them to blend in with their environment. This is called camouflage.

From a distance this tawny frogmouth is very hard to see because it looks like part of the tree.

Mob attack

Birds are not usually aggressive, but if an intruder threatens a group of birds, they may decide to attack it. The angry calls that they make as they attack act as a warning to other birds nearby.

These birds are mobbing a larger bird by calling and flapping their wings.

★

The last supper

For most animals, feasting on a hooded pitohui could be the last thing they do. These birds' feathers contain poison which can kill certain predators.

This doesn't help the pitohuis that have been eaten, but it means that other animals learn to leave these birds alone.

Hooded pitohuis are found in Papua New Guinea.

Acting sick

Birds sometimes put themselves at risk to protect their eggs and chicks. For example, a bird may pretend to be injured to attract a predator's attention. It can then lead the predator away from its nest.

This lesser golden plover is pretending its wing is broken to distract a predator.

Smelly creatures

Some birds use nasty smells to discourage predators. Common eiders squirt horrible-smelling chemicals onto their nests and northern fulmar chicks spit fish oil at intruders. New Guinea scrub fowls give off a smell like rotting meat when they are killed. This has led to people avoiding eating these birds.

Migration

Birds sometimes travel considerable distances to find food and places to breed, and to escape harsh weather conditions.

Svalbard barnacle geese breed in Svalbard and then fly to Scotland for the winter, where it is warmer.

Svalbard

Norway

Scotland

Breeding grounds

One reason that birds migrate is to travel to a particular area to lay eggs and bring up chicks. These areas are known as breeding grounds. Some birds travel hundreds of miles to return to the same breeding ground each year.

Day trippers

As well as making long journeys, some birds also make shorter, regular journeys each day. For example, zebra finches in the desert fly to water holes each day to drink.

Staying together

Many birds migrate in large groups for safety. Some fly in V-shaped formations. For the birds at the back of the group, this cuts down the amount of resistance as they travel through the air and saves them energy. The birds take turns in different positions in the group.

This group of Canada geese is migrating in a V-shaped formation. The birds make honking noises as they fly, so that they know where all the members of the group are.

The long, slender wings and forked tail of the Arctic tern are ideally suited to long distance flight.

Seeing the way

Nobody knows for certain how birds can find their way over such great distances. They may use landmarks such as mountains and rivers, or they may use the sun to help them find their way.

Long distance fliers

Arctic terns travel the furthest when they migrate. Twice each year they fly all the way from the Arctic to the Antarctic and back again. A one-way trip takes about four months.

They do this because it is summer in the Arctic when it is winter in the Antarctic and vice versa. By flying from one to the other, they can avoid the harshest, coldest weather conditions in each place.

Animal magnetism

The earth's core contains molten iron, which is magnetic. This creates a pull, or force, around the earth. Scientists think that there are some birds that use this force to guide them. This is particularly important for birds migrating at night.

The cutaway section of this globe shows different layers inside the earth.

This is the earth's magnetic core.

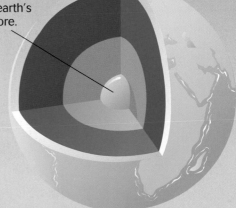

 ### Internet links

For links to websites where you can play a migration game, read the migration story of a golden plover and find out about other migrating birds, go to **www.usborne-quicklinks.com**

 Fact: Homing pigeons are known for their ability to find their way over long distances. They can fly up to 1,000km (over 600 miles) per day.

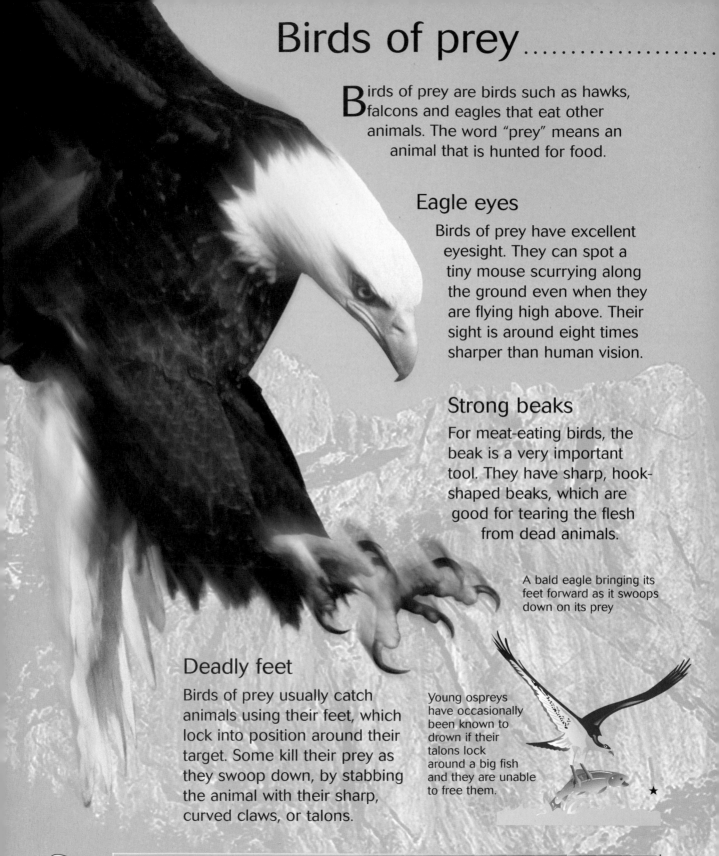

Birds of prey

Birds of prey are birds such as hawks, falcons and eagles that eat other animals. The word "prey" means an animal that is hunted for food.

Eagle eyes

Birds of prey have excellent eyesight. They can spot a tiny mouse scurrying along the ground even when they are flying high above. Their sight is around eight times sharper than human vision.

Strong beaks

For meat-eating birds, the beak is a very important tool. They have sharp, hook-shaped beaks, which are good for tearing the flesh from dead animals.

A bald eagle bringing its feet forward as it swoops down on its prey

Deadly feet

Birds of prey usually catch animals using their feet, which lock into position around their target. Some kill their prey as they swoop down, by stabbing the animal with their sharp, curved claws, or talons.

Young ospreys have occasionally been known to drown if their talons lock around a big fish and they are unable to free them.

Fact: The peregrine falcon is the fastest bird, diving after its prey at speeds of up to 180kph (110mph).

Dead meat

Vultures don't hunt for prey. Instead they eat animals that have died naturally or been killed by other animals.

Vultures have bald heads, so they can reach inside the bodies of dead animals to eat, without clogging their feathers with blood.

Ruppell's griffons have long necks which enable them to reach inside carcasses to pick clean the remains.

A bearded vulture soaring through the air looking for food

Hunting strategies

Birds of prey are skilful hunters. They use a wide range of methods to search for and attack their prey.

> ## Internet links
>
> For links to websites with information and webcam images of birds of prey, including eagles, falcons, vultures and owls, and their nests and chicks, go to **www.usborne-quicklinks.com**

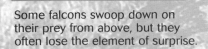

★ Secretary birds chase snakes along the ground, flapping their wings to try to confuse them.

★ Some falcons swoop down on their prey from above, but they often lose the element of surprise.

★ Some owls hunt from a still position. They try to stay hidden so they can catch their prey unaware.

Flightless birds 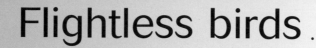 ....

All birds have wings, but not all of them can fly. The ones that live on the ground are easily attacked by other animals. They need to be able to swim or run quickly in order to survive.

Changing bodies

Flightless birds are probably descended from birds that used to fly. These may have lived in places where they had no predators, so it became safe to walk on the ground. Because they no longer used their wings, their bodies may have changed over many generations until they were no longer able to fly.

These ostriches are running in the Etosha National Park, Namibia. Ostriches can't fly, but they can run at speeds of up to 100kph (60mph).

Big birds

Ostriches are huge, flightless birds from Africa, with long necks and long, strong legs. They tower above most people, growing as tall as 2.5m (8ft). Their wings are very small in relation to their overall size. They use their wings to help them balance as they run.

Foot fight

Ostriches are fast runners and can easily outrun many predators. But they are also capable of putting up a good fight if they need to. They attack by kicking with both feet at the same time, and so are able to deliver very powerful kicks.

Living underground

Kiwis are strange flightless birds from New Zealand that live in burrows underground and only come out at night. This means that they avoid most of the animals that might want to harm them. Kiwis' straggly feathers make them look more like small furry animals than birds.

Kiwis probe for food on the forest floor. They have good hearing and an excellent sense of smell.

Taking to water

Penguins can't fly through air, but they can practically fly through water. They use their wings as paddles to propel themselves along.

Internet links

For links to websites where you can read about the evolution of flightless birds and find out about flightless birds today, and listen to a kiwi call or watch an ostrich video, go to
www.usborne-quicklinks.com

This is a Galapagos penguin swimming underwater. People often think of penguins as polar birds, but Galapagos penguins live near the equator.

Penguins have long, smooth bodies, which allow them to glide quickly through the water.

Penguins use their feet and tails to help them to change direction in the water.

Night birds

Most birds are active during the day and they sleep at night. But there are a few birds that are nocturnal, which means they come out at night.

Night owls

The best-known nocturnal birds are owls. They have extremely good sight and hearing, which help them to hunt for small animals at night.

Eyes forward

Unlike most birds, owls have eyes that face forward. This gives them a wider area of binocular vision than other birds, so they can focus well on fast-moving prey in the dark.

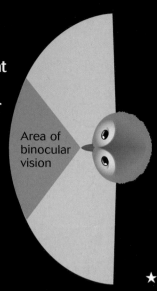

Area of binocular vision

The shaded areas show how far around an owl can see without moving its head.

A great horned owl turning its head to look behind it

These are just tufts of feathers, not ears.

The ears are hidden beneath the feathers.

Rotating head

Owls don't have as wide an area, or field, of vision as most birds. But they can rotate their heads so that they can look behind them.

All ears

Owls have round disks around their eyes with feathers shaped so that they channel sounds toward their ears. This improves their hearing.

Hide-and-seek

Many night birds have black and brown feathers, so they are hard to see when they are resting during the day.

Cave creatures

Oilbirds live in caves during the day and come out to hunt at night. They find their way around dark, narrow cave passages by making clicking noises.

The oilbird makes noises, which bounce off objects in its path.

When the bird hears the echo, it alters its path to avoid the obstacle. ★

Eye mirrors

Even when it is nearly dark, nightjars can make use of the little light there is. They have shiny layers at the backs of their eyes, which reflect light into the eyes to make the most of the light available. This makes their eyes look as though they are glowing in the dark.

Nightjars have bristles around their beaks which direct prey toward their mouths.

Waterbirds

Ponds, streams, rivers, lakes and seashores are home to many species of birds. These birds are well-suited to living in such watery places, which bird experts call wetlands.

Ducking under

Ducks swim along on the surface of the water, paddling with their webbed feet to propel themselves along. Sometimes you can just see a duck's bottom poking out of the water. This is when they are searching for food just below the water's surface.

A duck searching for food

Walking on water

Some lightweight waterbirds, such as jacanas and long-toed lapwings, can walk across floating plants. Their long toes help to spread their weight over a larger area, so they don't sink.

A jacana walking on plants floating on the water's surface

Fisher bird

Kingfishers often perch on branches overhanging rivers, on the lookout for fish to eat. When they see one, they dive into the water head first and grab the fish in their beaks.

This kingfisher is just about to plunge into the water to catch a fish.

Wading birds

Wading birds, such as plovers and curlews, live mainly in the muddy areas along seashores. They have long legs for walking in the sticky mud.

Pretty in pink

Flamingoes are bright pink birds that live in salty lakes. The tiny plants, or algae, that they eat contain chemicals called carotenoids. These are what make the birds' feathers pink. The same chemicals are found in carrots.

Long necks

Swans and geese have long necks which allow them to reach down to feed on vegetation that other waterbirds can't reach.

★ A swan feeding on vegetation

Internet links

For links to websites where you can zoom in on some waterbirds, find out about flamingoes and look for birds in an online wetland, go to **www.usborne-quicklinks.com**

The flamingo on the right is using its beak to filter food from the water.

Seabirds

Strong winds and storms make the open ocean a harsh environment for birds. However, many seabirds are strong fliers, capable of riding the winds and only rarely coming to land.

Puffins

Like penguins, puffins are good swimmers, but they can also fly. They have striking black and white feathers. During the breeding season, their beaks are bright red and blue, but they fade to a dull brown during the winter.

Puffins spend most of their time bobbing on the surface of the sea, occasionally diving to catch fish to eat. Their beaks have sharp edges, which help them to grip slippery fish.

Puffins have tiny spines on their beaks to enable them to hold several fish at once.

Food thieves

These skuas are making loud aggressive calls. They often do this to keep predators away from their nests.

Skuas are aggressive seabirds that steal most of their food from other birds. They chase and attack birds in the air until they drop their prey, or even regurgitate (bring back) food they have already eaten.

Easy pickings

Although gulls are seabirds, they are versatile, taking any opportunities to feed. They can often be seen following ships to feed on fish and other sea creatures that have been disturbed. However, they can also be found far inland, feeding on worms, small mammals and food that has been thrown away.

A flock of gulls flying close to the sea's surface in search of food

Internet links

For links to websites where you can visit a virtual puffin island, and find out more about gulls and other seabirds, go to **www.usborne-quicklinks.com**

Not land-lovers

European storm-petrels are one of the smallest seabirds. They are strong fliers, but they are so used to flying that on land they move awkwardly. Their legs can't support their weight, so they drag themselves around on their bellies, flapping their wings to help them move.

Amazing wings

Albatrosses are the largest seabirds. They have long, slender wings, which enable them to cover large distances by using air currents. The wandering albatross has the biggest wingspan of any bird, with each wing as long as a person is tall.

This diagram shows the wingspan of a wandering albatross.

3.6m (11.8ft)

Polar birds

A number of birds live in the icy areas around the North Pole (the Arctic) and the South Pole (the Antarctic). They have developed all kinds of ways of dealing with the cold.

This is the Arctic. It lies within the Arctic Circle, marked in red.

This is the Antarctic. It lies within the Antarctic Circle, marked in red.

Arctic seasons

In winter, the land and sea within the Arctic Circle are frozen, but in summer they warm up and some of the ice melts. Many birds spend the summer months in the Arctic, and then fly away when the winter comes.

Snow burrows

Snow buntings make burrows like this in the snow. ★

Snow buntings are small Arctic birds. They sometimes shelter from the freezing winds by burrowing in the snow.

Snow white

Some Arctic birds, such as snowy owls, snow geese and snow buntings, have white feathers to allow them to blend in with the snowy landscape.

The willow ptarmigan changes its feathers to suit the season. In winter it has white feathers, but as the snow melts, these are replaced with brown feathers, which blend in with the summer grasses and trees.

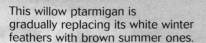

This willow ptarmigan is gradually replacing its white winter feathers with brown summer ones.

Antarctic penguins

In the Antarctic, the land is covered with snow and ice all year round. The best-known birds that live there are penguins. Several species live in the Antarctic, including emperor and Adelie penguins. Other penguins live in warmer waters further north.

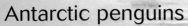

These Adelie penguins are diving into the sea head first, but as they jump out again, they keep their bodies upright.

Internet links

For links to websites where you can find out lots more about different species of penguins, pretend to be a penguin and find out how they communicate, go to **www.usborne-quicklinks.com**

Body heat

Penguins have a thick layer of fat, called blubber, beneath the skin which keeps them warm. They also have an outer layer of tightly-packed feathers to keep the heat in.

Huddling up

One way penguins keep warm is to huddle in groups. They take turns standing on the outside, where it is coldest, and then spend time in the middle of the group, where it is warmest.

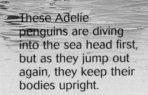

These young emperor penguins are huddling together for warmth.

Tropical birds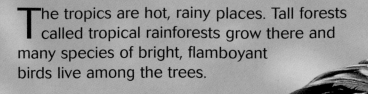

The tropics are hot, rainy places. Tall forests called tropical rainforests grow there and many species of bright, flamboyant birds live among the trees.

Bright but hidden

You may think that bright feathers would make birds easy to see. In fact, they help them to blend in with the vibrant flowers and dense, green leaves of the rainforests.

This yellow-headed parrot is from Costa Rica, Central America. It can balance on one leg while using its other foot to hold its food.

Clever birds

The best-known tropical birds are parrots. There are over 300 different species.

Parrots are intelligent, playful birds. Some have even been seen sliding down people's tents. In captivity, they have sometimes been taught to mimic human speech.

Handy feet

Parrots have flexible feet, which they use almost like hands. They can stand on one foot and pick things up with the other one.

They also have strong, hooked beaks, which are good for cracking open nuts. They use their beaks and feet together to help them eat.

 Fact: Around two-thirds of the world's bird species live in tropical rainforests.

Moody headgear

Cockatoos have strong, curved beaks, similar to those of parrots. They also have crests on their heads, which they can fan out to show when they are angry or frightened.

A palm cockatoo displaying its impressive crest

Rain dance

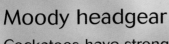

Cockatoos hang upside down like this to cool down in the rain.

★

When it rains after a dry spell, cockatoos sometimes perform a rain dance. They hang upside down with their wings stretched out, so that the water can cool the bare skin beneath.

Hummingbirds

Hummingbirds are tiny birds that feed on nectar, a sugary liquid produced by plants.

Hummingbirds get their name from the humming sound that their wings make because they flap them so quickly. This way of flying allows them to hover in front of plants while they are feeding.

This Costa's hummingbird is using its long, thin beak to reach inside a flower to feed on its nectar.

Desert birds

ot deserts are dry
places with little
shelter. The birds that
live in them have to
survive without much
water. During the
day it is very hot,
but at night it can
be freezing cold.

Water holes

Many birds, such as zebra
finches and cockatiels, need
to drink frequently. These
birds tend to gather near
water holes, often in large
groups. Water holes can be
dangerous places for smaller
birds, as animals often wait
there on the lookout for their
next meal. As a result, birds
drink in short bursts during
the hottest time of the day
when predators are resting.

Zebra finches get their name from
the black and white stripes, like a
zebra's, on their chests and tails.

Internet links

For links to websites where you can find
out more about how birds survive in
deserts and see photos and video clips
of birds in the Sahara Desert, go to
www.usborne-quicklinks.com

Water shortage

Because finding water
in the desert is so difficult,
some desert birds, such as
ostriches, vultures and
sociable weavers, have
developed the ability to go for
long periods of time without
drinking. Birds can also obtain
water from the foods they eat.

The houbara bustard's feathers blend in
well with the desert landscape. Like
many desert birds, it probably obtains
most of the water it needs from plants.

Spongy feathers

The Pallas' sandgrouse has an unusual way of collecting water so that it can transport it over long distances to its thirsty chicks.

The bird rubs the oil off its feathers and then plunges into water. The feathers soak up the water like a sponge.

Keeping cool

To keep cool during the hottest part of the day, many desert birds remain inactive or take shelter in rock crevices. If water is available they may take a bath.

This white-crowned black chat is carrying food to its nest hole.

Then it flies back to its chicks so that they can drink the water from its feathers.

Some birds, such as ostriches, expose bare parts of their bodies, such as under their wings, to lose heat from the bare skin. A few birds have a pouch called a gular sac beneath their chins which they vibrate to help them cool down.

Wanderers

Budgerigars live in large groups, sometimes containing thousands of birds. They can survive for up to five months without drinking, obtaining all the water they need from seeds. But usually they gather wherever there is plenty of food and water, moving on when the supplies run out. Birds that travel from place to place like this are described as nomadic.

Like most wild budgerigars, this one is mainly yellow and green. But budgerigars are sometimes kept as pets, and bred with blue feathers too.

Studying birds

The science of studying birds is called ornithology. Professional ornithologists have all kinds of ways of finding out about birds. But anyone can study the birds that they see every day just by watching them carefully.

Birdwatching

To study birds, you can join a young naturalists' group or just watch birds in a garden or local park. It's a good idea to go to the same place regularly, so you can see which birds gather there and how they behave at different times of the day or year.

These children are looking at birds in the Korup Rainforest in Cameroon.

Identifying birds

You can identify different species of birds by looking at their shapes and markings. However, many birds are very timid and it can be difficult to get a good view of them. Ornithologists often learn to identify birds by their songs and calls too.

The lesser grey shrike on the left and the great grey shrike on the right look so similar that you can only tell them apart by very careful observation.

Equipment

The basic equipment you need for birdwatching is a notebook, a pair of binoculars and a field guide containing pictures and descriptions to help you identify birds. Use the notebook to sketch birds and record information about them, such as size, markings, and beak shape. Always note when and where you see each bird.

A pair of lightweight binoculars like this is essential for birdwatching.

Endangered birds

One bird in serious danger of dying out is the kakapo, a flightless bird from New Zealand. Many flightless birds have already become extinct, because being unable to fly puts them at great risk of attack from predators.

Kakapos are flightless parrots.

Internet links

For links to websites where you can find out more about birds in danger and bird conservation projects, go to
www.usborne-quicklinks.com

People problems

Some species of birds have died out when people and domesticated animals moved into areas and hunted them for food. This has caused even very common birds to become extinct.

But one of the main ways that people harm hundreds of thousands of birds is through oil spills from tankers at sea. When birds' feathers become coated with oil, they are no longer waterproof and can become waterlogged, causing birds to drown.

Protecting birds

Conservation means looking after and managing the environment. Bird conservation aims to protect endangered birds, but it may also mean looking after more common species so that they don't become rare. It may involve bringing in laws to protect birds or setting up areas called reserves where birds and their environment are protected.

This oil-soaked bird has been rescued. If its feathers are cleaned, it may survive.

Amazing birds

Some birds have developed unusual characteristics or ways of behaving. This may be because they have adapted to living in a particular place. Sometimes we can only guess why birds have developed in this way.

Prehistoric birds

Hoatzin chicks have claws on their wings which they can use for climbing. Some ornithologists think that these claws mean the hoatzin is a link between modern birds and long-extinct animals, such as dinosaurs.

You can see the tiny claws on the wings of this hoatzin chick, which is hanging upside down.

A claw

Dancing displays

Cranes are known for their dancing displays. They sway, fan their wings and leap into the air. Dances may be performed by a pair of cranes or a whole group. Like a number of other birds, cranes sometimes dance to attract a mate, but they often seem to dance without a particular purpose.

Bizarre beak

The shoebill gets its name from its strange beak. The large beak with its hooked tip is ideal for catching fish, but it also has other uses. During courtship, the beak is snapped together to make a hollow sound to attract a mate. The bird also uses its beak to scoop water over its eggs to keep them cool.

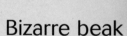
A shoebill

A pair of Japanese cranes dancing

This crane is leaping energetically into the air as part of its dance.

Loose legs

The gymnogene is a bird of prey with a special double joint in each of its legs that it can dislocate. During hunting, this allows it to reach inside rock crevices to catch reptiles and other prey.

★

A gymnogene dislocating its legs to reach into a hole

A nene (pronounced "nay-nay") raising one of its partially-webbed feet

Disappearing webs

The nene (or Hawaiian goose) lives on the slopes of volcanoes in Hawaii. It is unusual because it is the only goose with feet that are just partially webbed. It has adapted to living in high volcanic areas, where there is little water and no need for fully webbed feet.

Record breakers

Some birds are graceful fliers, while others can't fly at all. Some can run very quickly, but others can't even walk. There are birds that are taller than people, but many can fit in a person's hand. On these pages, you can find out some amazing bird facts.

- Ostriches are the tallest and heaviest birds. They reach a height of around 2.5m (8ft) and weigh up to 156.5kg (350lbs).

- The tallest birds ever to have lived are giant moas. They are now extinct, but they probably grew to over 3m (10ft) tall.

- Bee hummingbirds are the smallest birds. They are smaller than bumblebees and weigh just 1.6g (0.06oz).

- Australian pelicans have the longest beaks – around 45cm (18in) long.

- Nightjars have the shortest beaks – around 1cm (0.4in) long.

- The biggest eggs are laid by ostriches. They are around 17.8cm (7.1in) long and 14cm (5.6in) wide, which is around two-thirds the size of a soccer ball.

- The smallest eggs are laid by bee hummingbirds. They are just 0.64cm (0.25in) long.

- The largest tree-nests built by a single bird are those of bald eagles. The nests are around 2.9m (9.5ft) wide and 6m (19.7ft) deep – big enough to fit several people inside.

- The smallest nests are built by vervain hummingbirds. They are about 1.5cm (0.6in) across, which is about the width of a person's thumbnail.

The Australian pelican has the longest beak.

- When a woodpecker strikes a tree with its beak, it does so at a speed of 40kph (25mph).

- Wandering albatrosses have the greatest wingspan of any bird. When their wings are fully stretched, the distance between the tips of the wings can be up to 3.6m (11.8ft).

- Ruby-throated hummingbirds have the least feathers, with less than 1,000.

- Peregrine falcons can fly faster than any other bird. When they plunge down after their prey, they can reach speeds of up to 180kph (112mph).

- Gentoo penguins are the fastest-swimming birds, reaching speeds of around 27kph (17mph).

- Ostriches are the fastest-running birds. They can reach speeds of up to 97kph (60mph).

- It is estimated that during a display hummingbirds can flap their wings up to 200 times per second.

- Some of the largest birds live the longest. For example, wandering albatrosses can live for around 80 years, which is as long as most people live.

- Owls have fringes on the edges of their wings so they are able to fly almost silently.

- Arctic terns have the longest annual migration of any bird. They fly 36,000km (22,320 miles) from the Arctic to the Antarctic and back again.

- The bird with the most feathers is the North American whistling swan, or tundra swan, which has over 25,000.

Although the tundra swan is not the biggest bird, it does have the most feathers.

- There are one-quarter as many red-billed queleas as there are people in the world. They are the most common bird, with a total of 1.5 thousand million.

- The nests of cave swiftlets are used to make bird's-nest soup, which is a popular dish in China. The nests are made from plant material and the birds' saliva.

- Grey partridges lay the most eggs in one clutch – up to 19.

- Emperor penguins can stay underwater for as long as 18 minutes without coming up for air.

- African grey parrots can learn up to 800 words, about the same number of words that a three-year-old child uses.

Internet links

Throughout this book we have recommended websites where you can find out more about birds. To visit the sites, go to the **Usborne Quicklinks Website** where you will find links to all the sites.

1. Go to **www.usborne-quicklinks.com**
2. Type the keywords for this book: **discovery birds**
3. Type the page number of the link you want to visit.
4. Click on the link to go to the recommended site.

Here are some of the things you can do on the websites recommended in this book:
• Watch animations showing how birds fly.
• Identify different types of bird call.
• Play a nest identification game.
• View webcam images of birds of prey.
• Dissect a virtual owl pellet.

Site availability

The links in Usborne Quicklinks are regularly reviewed and updated, but occasionally you may get a message that a site is unavailable. This might be temporary, so try again later, or even the next day. Websites do occasionally close down and when this happens, we will replace them with new links in Usborne Quicklinks. Sometimes we add extra links too, if we think they are useful. So when you visit Usborne Quicklinks, the links may be slightly different from those described in your book.

Downloadable pictures

Pictures marked with a ★ in this book can be downloaded from the Usborne Quicklinks Website. These pictures are for personal use only and must not be used for commercial purposes.

> COMPUTER NOT ESSENTIAL
> If you don't have access to the internet, don't worry. This book is a fun and informative introduction to birds.

Safety on the internet

Ask your parent's or guardian's permission before you connect to the internet and make sure you follow these simple rules:

• Never give out information about yourself, such as your real name, address, phone number or the name of your school.
• If a site asks you to log in or register by typing your name or email address, ask permission from an adult first.

What you need

To visit the websites you need a computer with an internet connection and a web browser (the software that lets you look at information from the internet). Some sites need extra programs (plug-ins) to play sound or show videos or animations.

If you go to a site and do not have the necessary plug-in, a message will come up on the screen. There is usually a link to click on to download the plug-in. For more information about plug-ins, go to Usborne Quicklinks and click on "Net Help".

Notes for parents and guardians

The websites described in this book are regularly reviewed, but the content of a website may change at any time and Usborne Publishing is not responsible for the content on any website other than its own.

We recommend that children are supervised while on the Internet, that they do not use internet chat rooms, and that you use internet filtering software to block unsuitable material. Please ensure that your children read and follow the safety guidelines printed above. For more information, see the Net Help area on the Usborne Quicklinks Website.

Index ···

····························· 63

Acknowledgements ....

Every effort has been made to trace the copyright holders of the material in this book. If any rights have been omitted, the publishers offer to rectify this in any subsequent editions following notification. The publishers are grateful to the following organizations and individuals for their permission to reproduce material (t=top, m=middle, b=bottom, l=left, r=right):

Cover © NHPA/John Shaw, © Digital Vision; **p1** © Digital Vision; **p2** © Digital Vision; **p3** © Stockbyte; **p4** (background) © Digital Vision, (main) © Digital Vision; **p5** (t) © Kim Taylor/Bruce Coleman, (bl) © George McCarthy/Bruce Coleman, (br) © Digital Vision; **p6** © Clive Druett; Papilio/CORBIS; **p7** © Roger Tidman/CORBIS; **p8** © Kim Taylor/Bruce Coleman; **p9** © Kevin Schafer/CORBIS; **p10** (background) © Digital Vision, (t) © NHPA/ Stephen Dalton; **p11** © NHPA/Stephen Dalton; **p12** (l) © Digital Vision, (r) © Digital Vision; **p13** © Niall Benvie/ CORBIS; **p14** (bl) © Staffan Widstrand/Bruce Coleman, (tr) © Tim Zurowski/CORBIS, (mr) © Darrell Gulin/CORBIS, (br) © John Cancalosi/Bruce Coleman; **p15** (mr) © Mike Read, (b) © Warren Photographic/Kim Taylor; **p16** (tl) © Xavier Eichaker/Still Pictures, (mr and br) © Alain Compost/Bruce Coleman; **p17** © Digital Vision; **p18** © Michael S. Yamashita/CORBIS; **p19** (t and b) © Wolfgang Kaehler/CORBIS; **p20** (tr) © Chris Gomersall/Bruce Coleman, (bl) © Michael McKavett/Bruce Coleman; **p21** (t) © Michael McKavett/Bruce Coleman, (b) © Chris Mattison; Frank Lane Picture Agency/CORBIS; **p22** (bl) © Bill Coster/Windrush, (r) © HPH Photography/Bruce Coleman; **p23** (tr) © Luiz Claudio Marigo/Bruce Coleman, (br) © Digital Vision; **p24** (tr) © M. P. L. Fogden/Bruce Coleman, (bl) © George Lepp/CORBIS; **p25** (tr) © John Cancalosi/Bruce Coleman, (bl) © NHPA/E. A. Janes; **p26** © Jane Burton/Bruce Coleman; **p27** (tr) © Jane Burton/Bruce Coleman, (b) © Digital Vision; **p28** (tr) © NHPA/Roger Tidman, (b) © Digital Vision; **p29** © Jonathan Blair/CORBIS; **p30** (bl) © Peter Johnson/CORBIS, (r) © Charles O'Rear/CORBIS; **p31** (tr) © James L. Amos/CORBIS (br) © Fritz Polking; Frank Lane Picture Agency/CORBIS; **p32** © Peter Johnson/CORBIS; **p33** © Digital Vision; **p34** © Jen & Des Bartlett/Bruce Coleman; **p35** (tr) © NHPA/Hellio & Van Ingen, (br) © NHPA/Daniel Heuclin; **p36** © Chase Swift/CORBIS; **p37** © James L. Amos/ CORBIS; **p38** (background) © Digital Vision (tl) © Bruce Coleman Inc.; **p39** (tl) © Digital Vision, (tr) © Dr P. Evans/ Bruce Coleman; **p40** (l) © Wolfgang Kaehler/CORBIS, (m) © Jen and Des Bartlett/Bruce Coleman; **p41** (tr) © Gerald S. Cubitt/Bruce Coleman, (b) © NHPA/Norbert Wu; **p42** © Tim Zurowski/CORBIS; **p43** © Gary Higgins/ Windrush; **p44** (l) © NHPA/Silvestris fotoservice, (br) © Peter Johnson/CORBIS; **p45** © Digital Vision; **p46** (tr) © Eric and David Hosking/CORBIS, (b) © Mike Buxton; Papilio/CORBIS; **p47** © Amos Nachoum/CORBIS; **p48** © Stephen J. Krasemann/Bruce Coleman; **p49** (tr) © Michael Gore/Windrush, (b) © David Tipling/Windrush; **p50** © Konrad Wothe/Bruce Coleman; **p51** (bl) © Bob & Clara Calhoun/Bruce Coleman, (r) © Alain Compost/Bruce Coleman; **p52** (tl) © Hans Reinhard/Bruce Coleman, (b) © Eric and David Hosking/CORBIS; **p53** (tr) © Eric and David Hosking/CORBIS, (br) © Jane Burton/Bruce Coleman; **p54** (bl) © Gilles Nicolet/Still Pictures, (br) Image provided by Minolta (UK) Limited; **p55** (tr) © Sandro Vannini/CORBIS, (bl) © John Quinn, Oxford University; **p56** (tr) © Mr P. Clement/Bruce Coleman, (bl) © The Purcell Team/CORBIS; **p57** (tr) © Gerald S. Cubitt/Bruce Coleman, (br) © AFP/CORBIS; **p58** (bl) © Kevin Schafer/CORBIS, (main) © Bruce Coleman/Orion Press; **p59** © James L. Amos/CORBIS; **p60** (background) © Stockbyte, (bl) © Michael Maconachie; Papilio/CORBIS; **p61** (tr) © Lowell Georgia/CORBIS

Managing editor: Jane Chisholm; Managing designer: Mary Cartwright; Photographic manipulation: John Russell and Andrea Slane; Cover design: Helen Edmonds; Additional designs by Nicola Butler; Additional consultant: Dr. Mark O'Connell, Wildfowl and Wetlands Trust; With thanks to U.S. expert Daniel King.